Secret Schools

True Stories of the Determination to Learn

WRITTEN BY HEATHER CAMLOT ILLUSTRATED BY ERIN TANIGUCHI

Owlkids Books

For Sharlene: my schoolmate, my neighbor, my first reader, my friend — H.C.

This book wouldn't be possible without editor Stacey Roderick, who secretly schools me in the art of nonfiction writing for children; Owlkids Books publisher Karen Boersma and former editorial director Karen Li for being so embracing of my ideas; the whole Owlkids team for all the work they do getting books into readers' hands; Erin Taniguchi for their incredible linocut illustrations; designer Danielle Arbour for her stellar layout; copy editor Kelly Hope for her keen eye; my friends Marsha Moshinsky for translating Spanish documents and Sharlene Wiseman for her first read; my husband, Marc, and my children, Alex and Juliana, for cheering me on; and my parents, who made no secret of their belief in the importance of school.

To my parents, Sue and Ron, for supporting my artistic journey — E.T.

Text © 2022 Heather Camlot
Illustrations © 2022 Erin Taniguchi

Owlkids Books acknowledges the financial support of the Canada Council for the Arts, the Ontario Arts Council, the Government of Canada through the Canada Book Fund (CBF) and the Government of Ontario through the Ontario Creates Book Initiative for our publishing activities.

Published in Canada by
Owlkids Books Inc.
1 Eglinton Avenue East
Toronto, ON M4P 3A1

Published in the United States by
Owlkids Books Inc.
1700 Fourth Street
Berkeley, CA 94710

Library of Congress Control Number: 2021951241

Library and Archives Canada Cataloguing in Publication

Title: Secret schools : true stories of the determination to learn / written by Heather Camlot ;
    illustrated by Erin Taniguchi.
Names: Camlot, Heather, author. | Taniguchi, Erin, illustrator.
Description: Includes bibliographical references and index.
Identifiers: Canadiana 20210382732 | ISBN 9781771474603 (hardcover)
Subjects: LCSH: Right to education—Juvenile literature. | LCSH: Education—Juvenile literature. |
    LCSH: Education—Social aspects—Juvenile literature.
Classification: LCC LC213 .C36 2022 | DDC j379.2/6—dc23

Edited by Stacey Roderick
Designed by Danielle Arbour

Manufactured in Guangdong Province, Dongguan City, China, in March 2022, by Toppan Leefung Packaging & Printing (Dongguan) Co., Ltd.   Job #BAYDC107

A   B   C   D   E   F   G

Publisher of Chirp, Chickadee and OWL
www.owlkidsbooks.com | Owlkids Books is a division of bayard canada

Contents

Introduction

What if it meant leaving your home late at night so no one knew where you were going? Or hiding from the government or members of your family? Or risking imprisonment—and even death?

Can you keep a secret?

What if the secret was that you were going to *school*?

Secret Schools is a peek into underground education and the hidden classrooms that opened their doors so children and adults could learn, even when it was illegal. You'll see how far many people have gone—and are still going—to feed their need for knowledge, to prepare for a better future, to carry on their cultural heritage, and to protect their country and fellow citizens.

Each section in this book explores one of the many reasons why people have turned to a secret education. You'll read about enslaved people in the United States, European Jews, and South African political prisoners whose studies allowed them to be free in mind if not in body. You'll learn how communities around the world used secret schools to hold on to their language and cultural identity. You'll be introduced to women who refused to let the ruling authorities of their countries deny them an education just because of their gender. You'll discover three historic secret-agent training facilities—schools that had to be kept secret from the public and, more importantly, from the enemy. Finally, you'll learn about under-the-radar alternative schooling offered by a billionaire in the United States, by students in South Korea, and by the government of Indonesia.

Some of the reasons behind these secret schools might surprise you. Others you might understand quite well. And some you may disagree with. But for all who attended these secret schools, covert classes were the best—if not the only—option for the education that they wanted or needed.

1

CULTURAL
CONNECTIONS

PROTECTING ONE'S
IDENTITY

The language we learn as our native tongue isn't just a way for us to speak to our family and friends. It's also a connection to our community and culture. Japanese migrant workers in Brazil, Indigenous peoples in Ecuador, and Lithuanians living under Russian rule all refused to let authorities stamp out their language. Instead, they created secret schools to teach their languages—and made their cultural identities even stronger.

The fine print

Under the cover of night, smugglers snuck back into Lithuania, careful to avoid the border guards and Russian police. If caught, they could be whipped, shot, imprisoned, or sent to live in remote Siberia. And yet for some forty years, people would risk these punishments to bring their fellow citizens one essential thing: the books needed to secretly teach Lithuanian history, culture, and language.

In 1863, the people of Lithuania had tried to rise up against ruling Tsarist Russia, but failed. The Tsarist authorities struck back by banning Lithuanian-language schools and the printing of Lithuanian books. The idea: to force the country into embracing Russian ideals and culture.

But this tactic led to more resistance.

A Lithuanian bishop, Motiejus Valančius, helped set up a network of underground schools throughout the country so that teachers could continue to teach the Lithuanian language. Mothers secretly taught their children to read and write Lithuanian at home. Any children still attending Russian state schools were constantly reminded by their families that their secret Lithuanian lessons were their *real* lessons.

But all this secret teaching required books that were written in Lithuanian. Valančius wrote some books to fill the need and sent money to neighboring East Prussia to build a special printing press. Thousands of book smugglers—some of whom didn't know how to read or write themselves—snuck in textbooks, almanacs, and whatever else they could. Millions of books made their way into Lithuania, even from the United States, thousands of miles and an ocean away.

The Lithuanian secret schools—which were active in practically every village and town—not only helped maintain culture but also pushed the country's literacy rate to one of the highest in Tsarist Russia!

The ban on Lithuanian literature was lifted in 1904 when the Russian Empire finally accepted that its plan had failed. (It also wanted its territories to be loyal during its war with Japan.) The next year, former book smuggler Juozas Masiulis opened a bookstore—the J. Masiulio Knygynas—lawfully providing books to all those who had been secretly taught Lithuanian and who had maintained their language during the darkest days. The bookstore still exists today.

After working with Bishop Valančius, smuggler Jurgis Bielinis went on to form one of the largest book smuggling operations in Lithuania, the Garšviai Book Smuggling Society. Bielinis and his fellow smugglers used their own money to buy books, including textbooks and novels, in East Prussia and distributed them throughout the country. His contribution to the country's fight to keep its language is considered so important that Lithuanians celebrate *Knygnešio diena*, or Day of the Book Carrier, every March 16—Bielinis's birthday.

A world apart

The Japanese migrant workers were very far from home when their ship docked in Santos, Brazil, on June 18, 1908. Many in this first wave of workers from Japan hoped to earn money working on coffee plantations and then return home soon after. But they quickly learned that saving while working for someone else was nearly impossible.

When the opportunity to rent or buy their own land came up, many migrant workers jumped at it. Soon, Japanese migrant communities formed, and schools teaching the Japanese language—which the migrants' children would need when they returned to their homeland—were built. Some of the students were also taught Portuguese, the national language of Brazil.

By 1930, some one hundred thousand Japanese had immigrated to Brazil. In that year, a new government came into power, fueling a racist, anti-Japanese

attitude; within the decade, teaching foreign languages to children under fourteen years old was banned. This forced hundreds of Japanese schools to close, affecting about thirty thousand children of Japanese descent.

But that didn't stop the Japanese migrants from educating their children. Instead, the schooling moved underground: parents secretly taught Japanese language and culture at home, and former teachers moved from place to place, holding classes hidden in shacks or garages. During this time, the children were scared of being reported to the authorities. And rightfully so: sometimes Brazilian neighbors would tip off the government when they saw a handful of children together, assuming it meant a Japanese class was in session.

Things went from bad to worse during World War II, when Brazil and Japan supported opposite sides of the conflict. The people of Japanese descent living in Brazil were essentially treated like enemies. The government forbade them to meet in groups, foreign-language press was banned, Japanese literature was seized, and speaking in Japanese was restricted to inside the home. Some were arrested as suspected spies and others had their money and property taken away. Still, the underground Japanese schooling

managed to continue, even though families had to hide their teaching materials by burying them and Japanese language teachers would be arrested if found teaching.

When the war ended in 1945, Japan was in ruins. Many people of Japanese descent decided to stay in Brazil. Teaching the Japanese language was allowed again and the secrecy was no longer necessary. Knowing Japanese remained important to the community, but a Brazilian education became a focus for those who stayed in Brazil permanently. Today, Brazil is home to more Japanese descendants than any other country in the world.

When the island nation of Okinawa was taken over by Japan in 1879, the Okinawan language was banned. About 40 percent of the Japanese immigrants to Brazil in 1908 were from Okinawa, and they chose to speak their banned language in their new country. Like the migrants from the Japanese mainland, they also established communities and secret schools in Brazil, making it possible for their specific culture and language to be handed down to future generations.

Mother tongue

Ecuador's wealthy landowners didn't believe the children of Indigenous families living on their large estates, called haciendas, needed an education. Although Ecuador had become independent from Spain in 1822, the landowners, who were of Spanish descent, remained very powerful. Under the hacienda system, the landless Indigenous workers lived on and farmed small plots of land in exchange for their labor. For the workers, that meant very low pay, long hours, and sometimes even physical abuse.

By Ecuadorian law, Indigenous children living on haciendas had to attend school, either near or on the hacienda itself. But since landowners made more money when the children worked, some refused to build schools while others made sure the children were turned away from the local one.

The Indigenous children who did attend school were taught European values and the Spanish language, rather than their own. This didn't sit well with Indigenous activist Dolores Cacuango, who was also known as Mamá Dulu. Fearing Indigenous languages, cultures, and values would be lost over time, she tried to convince authorities to provide an Indigenous education. Her attempts were completely ignored, but not one to give up, she decided to start her own underground school in the mid-1940s.

Although illiterate herself, Cacuango and a teacher named María Luisa Gómez de la Torre began secretly teaching classes in Cacuango's hometown of Cayambe. Lessons had to happen at night, after the children had finished a day of work on the hacienda. In the beginning, classes were held in people's homes, moving from hut to hut on the hacienda. So that no one hut would draw suspicion, all the huts kept their lights on while lessons ran. Some huts had double walls that could hide a classroom or had desks that could be taken apart quickly in case someone came poking around.

These students were secretly taught their ancestral Kichwa language *and* Spanish. That's because Cacuango believed that to stand up for yourself, you need to be able to communicate directly with the people in power, not through translators or interpreters.

With the support of Indigenous rights and feminist organizations, Cacuango was eventually able to set up four rural schools in Cayambe. As a result, Cacuango was repeatedly harassed and hounded, and the students and parents were intimidated. The government continually tried to close the schools, but Cacuango and colleagues fought back. When a new military government seized control of Ecuador in 1963, it shut down the last

of the rural schools for good, sending Kichwa education back underground.

But the desire to preserve and teach Indigenous languages and cultures continued. In 1988, the Ecuadorian government finally agreed to a second public school system in which Indigenous children are taught Indigenous cultures and languages as well as Spanish—an approach inspired by the underground schooling Dolores Cacuango began more than forty years earlier.

Dolores Cacuango was born on a hacienda in 1881. Because her parents were in debt, she worked as a domestic servant for the landowner. There she saw how differently the landowners and the Indigenous peoples lived, and dedicated herself to the fight for Indigenous rights. One priority was education: "Just as the sun shines equally for all men and women; so should education shine on all, rich or poor, lords or servants," she said. She died in 1971 but today is remembered as a pioneer in education.

2

HOPE AND DIGNITY

ESCAPING SLAVERY AND OPPRESSION

People kidnapped from their African homelands and enslaved. Jewish people rounded up in ghettos and concentration camps. Black South Africans imprisoned for fighting to end apartheid. Around the world and throughout history, people have been oppressed simply because of their skin color, religion, or beliefs. For some, secret schools became a way to escape mentally, if not physically.

From literacy to liberty

In the 1700s and 1800s, enslavers living in British North America were so worried about the possibility of enslaved people learning to read and write that they did everything they could to prevent it.

Beginning in the 1600s, hundreds of thousands of people were kidnapped from African countries and sold as forced, unpaid labor for a wide range of work in what would become the United States of America. These enslaved people were considered the property of the people they worked for.

Their enslavers worried that if the enslaved people were literate, they would communicate with each other through writing, read about abolition (the movement to end slavery), and learn about others who had escaped to freedom. Essentially, the enslavers feared literacy would lead to rebellion and resistance, which were already happening in subtle ways every day. So when word got out that some enslaved people were learning to read and write, laws were made to forbid it.

Many enslaved people saw literacy as a path to freedom and risked the severe punishments. According to the law, Black students could be whipped; their Black teachers could be fined, imprisoned, or whipped; and their white teachers could be imprisoned or made to pay hefty fines. Then there were the enslavers who took the law into their own hands, issuing punishments ranging from beatings to death.

As an enslaved child, Frederick Douglass was sent to a married couple in Baltimore, Maryland. There, the wife secretly taught him to read and write. Her husband was furious when he found out, believing Douglass would become unmanageable as an enslaved person. "Knowledge unfits a child to be a slave," Douglass would later write. "From that moment I understood the direct pathway from slavery to freedom." Knowing then how powerful literacy was, Douglass read everything he could. As a teenager, he began secretly teaching other enslaved people to read and write—he even had as many as forty students in a Sunday class. At age twenty, Douglass escaped to freedom and became a prominent abolitionist, human rights leader, and author.

Some enslaved people were taught by religious societies or by their enslavers who (knowingly and unknowingly) defied the laws. But others found clever and courageous ways to learn. For example, secret schools were run out of the homes of freed Black people, lessons were taught at night in secluded cabins or dug-out pits covered with vines, and classes were held on Sundays when the enslavers were at church.

It all took careful planning, whispered messages, and concealed communication to make sure they weren't discovered. Students would take roundabout routes to reach their secret destinations one at a time, making sure no one saw them enter the "classroom." They hid their schoolbooks, often by wrapping them in paper. If they didn't have school supplies, they wrote letters in the dirt with sticks or on bark using ink made from oak trees.

Thanks to these secret schools and teachers, a number of enslaved people were able to escape north to freedom by writing their own travel pass and signing their enslaver's name. Others became teachers themselves and taught those

around them. One secret-school teacher, Lilly Ann Granderson, would go on to help establish a seminary in Mississippi to train Black teachers and ministers. The school, later renamed Jackson State University, still exists today.

A mental escape

Overcrowding, hunger, disease, brutality: those were just some of the horrendous conditions faced by Jewish people forced to live in ghettos during World War II. As part of the Holocaust, more than one thousand ghettos had been set up by German authorities to separate Jews from non-Jews in villages and towns across occupied Eastern Europe. Germany's leader, Adolf Hitler, wanted Jewish people to be "removed" because he blamed them for the country's defeat in World War I and for all the country's problems.

Educating Jewish children was also banned and anyone caught teaching or learning in the ghettos could be killed. Despite this, members of the Jewish community set up secret schools: kindergartens and elementary and secondary schools where students were taught Hebrew, history, geography, art, and more. Depending on the age of the children, lessons took the form of songs, stories, and even games. There were also underground yeshivas where students focused on religious studies.

Judaism has long been a culture of learning, but in the ghettos, schools were also a refuge. They were a way to keep children safely off the streets and a way to keep life a little bit normal. Hidden classrooms were set up in soup kitchens, stables, attics—wherever teachers could find a spot away from prying eyes. Some children brought their books concealed under their clothes.

These teachers and their lessons gave students hope, humanity, and a

Jews rounded up in Hronov, Czechoslovakia (now Czech Republic), in December 1942 were allowed to pack no more than 110 lb. (50 kg). Artist and art therapist Friedl Dicker-Brandeis filled her two suitcases mainly with art supplies. Sent to the Theresienstadt ghetto, she secretly taught art to hundreds of children living there. Art gave them the freedom to dream, to imagine, to remember—and to document their lives. In fall 1944, Dicker-Brandeis refilled her two suitcases with five thousand pieces of artwork and hid them. Shortly after, she and some of her students were boarded onto a train to their deaths at the Auschwitz-Birkenau camp. Their artwork, however, lives on at the Jewish Museum in Prague.

form of resistance. Regardless of what they learned or how they learned it, the clandestine schools helped give students a feeling of what their lives used to be like. They were places to forget about the hunger in their bellies and the madness inside and outside the ghetto walls.

As the war progressed, Jews were taken from the ghettos and elsewhere and sent either to death camps to be immediately murdered or to concentration camps where they and other prisoners were forced to live and work in inhumane conditions. But even amid the devastation, some adults ran secret classes for the children, despite having only a handful of books to use. There they filled young minds with stories—until the very end.

Freedom of thought

In the shark-infested waters off South Africa's coast, Robben Island's maximum-security prison held more than three thousand political prisoners between 1961 and 1991. Their crime? Fighting to end the oppression, segregation, and white-minority rule that defined the country's apartheid era.

Some of the political prisoners, all of whom were Black and people of color, had never been taught to read and write; others were schoolteachers and university graduates. Famous freedom fighter Nelson Mandela and other educated political prisoners took it upon themselves to teach all their fellow prisoners in secret: they vowed that no one jailed on the island would leave without being able to read and write. They also offered a political education to anyone who wanted it. They called it the University of Robben Island.

How did this happen under the watchful eyes of the guards? Sometimes prisoners gathered in a nearby limestone cave during their breaks from cutting stone under the glaring sun, writing lessons in the dirt the way a classroom teacher would write on a chalkboard. Other times prisoners quietly broke into clandestine clusters for discussions and lectures while they worked—the topic whatever that "lecturer" was knowledgeable in, from history to economics. Some lessons were sent as secret notes to prisoners in other sections. Amazingly, within three to four years, illiteracy among prisoners was wiped out.

Still, all this teaching and studying was risky. Robben Island was a harsh place for all the prisoners sent there. But for the political prisoners, it was especially difficult and often brutal, both physically and mentally. They already had no beds, limited and censored mail, minimal clothing and food, news blackouts, and no chance for parole. Meanwhile, anything that bothered the white warden and guards could lead them to mistreat the prisoners, with reprimands ranging from "teachers" losing whatever study privileges they might have had to meals being taken away, solitary confinement, and physical punishment. Studies and

conversations were what kept hope and the human spirit alive.

A number of Robben Island's political prisoners went on to use their education to help their country end apartheid so that all South African citizens would be treated equally.

Mandela, who studied for a Bachelor of Laws degree on the island, went on to become South Africa's first democratically elected and first Black president. "Education," he said, "is the most powerful weapon which you can use to change the world."

It wasn't always against the rules to study at the Robben Island prison. It depended on who was in charge at the time. But taking away study privileges was continually used as a threat and punishment. Still, many prisoners studied for their high school equivalencies. They and some other prisoners also took university correspondence courses and graduated with one or more degrees! Nelson Mandela even insisted the guards pursue higher education. Without the top authorities' knowledge, some prisoners and guards studied together and shared books, while older educated prisoners helped guards with their assignments.

3

GIRLS' RIGHTS

BANDING TOGETHER
FOR GENDER EQUALITY

Whether stealing away to lectures under the cover of night, pretending to take socially acceptable classes, or simply not explaining their activities at all, women and girls over the course of history have refused to be denied an education just because of their gender. Instead, they boldly set up and attended secret schools despite orders from government, militants, and even their own families.

Taking flight

In 1882, women stepped into the dark streets of Warsaw, Poland, to carefully make their way to the homes secretly hosting lectures and seminars led by the country's great academic and intellectual minds. To be discovered by police could mean prison or exile to Siberia for the teachers and students.

Why would they take such a risk? It was part of an underground rebellion.

Poland had lost its independence to Russia, Prussia, and Austria in 1795. Yet the Polish people organized a series of revolts. Although the revolts failed, the governing powers decided to tighten their control. Over time, that came to include banning Polish studies like history and language as a way to wipe out feelings of national pride. For women, university was completely banned.

So beginning in 1882, teacher Jadwiga Szczawińska-Dawidowa and others responded by organizing clandestine classes for women in Warsaw to study Polish language and literature. Demand grew, and in 1886 she organized the classes into the formal yet secret Flying University—so-called because students constantly "flew" from one concealed location to another to avoid detection.

The classes ranged from math and science to history and philosophy. Over time, some classes moved out of private homes and were hidden behind closed doors of institutions and museums that supported the cause. Because Flying University's education wasn't restricted or censored like the country's foreign-controlled universities, men soon wanted to attend, too. The secret doors opened to them, but women always made up the majority of students.

Two of Flying University's most famous students were Marie Curie (born Maria Skłodowska) and Janusz Korczak (born Henryk Goldszmit). Curie pioneered research in radioactivity and became the first person and only woman to win the Nobel Prize twice. Korczak was a Jewish doctor and author who died in 1942 at the Treblinka death camp alongside the two hundred orphans in his care whom he had refused to abandon to save his own life.

Thousands of students had secretly attended classes through Flying University by the time the government allowed it to operate openly—first as the Society for Scientific Courses and then as the Free Polish University—after the Russian Revolution of 1905. However, Flying University's undercover approach was so successful that it was also used when schools were closed during World War II and then again as part of the resistance to state-controlled education between 1977 and 1981.

After invading Poland in 1939, the Germans forbade Polish education in an attempt to destroy the culture. Most schools were shut down. Some teachers were arrested, deported, or killed. Some went into hiding. Inspired by Flying University, the Secret Teaching Organization was formed as a massive underground education network that taught some one million children during World War II.

Opening doors

An "open secret" is an oxymoron—two words together that contradict each other. But an open secret is just what Iran's Taraqqi Girls' School was.

In the early 1900s, women in Iran formed secret societies to fight for national reforms and a new constitution. Together, they joined demonstrations, refused to buy foreign fabrics, and even sold their own jewelry to help finance a national bank. But when the country's first constitution was signed in 1906, the rights of women—who had worked so tirelessly for change—were completely ignored. They complained and were told, "Women's education and training should be restricted to raising children, home economics, and preserving the honor of the family."

That didn't go over very well. Women took action—by turning their already organized and powerful attention to women's rights and girls' education. With a few exceptions, Muslim girls didn't attend school at that time. (There weren't many education opportunities for them.) In the capital city of Tehran in 1907, members of one secret society held an important meeting where they resolved to create Muslim girls' schools, as well as to banish dowries (money a bride's family pays to a husband) and use those funds for girls' education instead.

The first of these schools for Muslim girls opened in 1907. The government knew about its opening and the opening of dozens of other girls' schools in and outside Tehran, but it wouldn't help them financially. To keep the schools going, individual

Iran is home to millions of Afghan refugees who fled their homeland and crossed the border to escape violence and insecurity in their country. Without legal status, a place in a state school was not guaranteed. (As of 2019, as many as two million refugees, including hundreds of thousands of children, still don't have their registration papers.) School fees and other policies also made attendance difficult. In response, people set up secret classrooms. Teachers and students were constantly on the lookout for patrolling police who had no problem shutting down the underground operations. Things improved in 2015, however, when the country's supreme leader, Ayatollah Ali Khamenei, ordered all children—regardless of status—to attend school.

women made donations and women's groups raised money. Nor would the government protect the teachers and students from people who opposed the schools and who believed that anyone involved was sinful and morally corrupt. Young girls were pelted with stones, teachers were attacked, and schools were looted.

Though she herself had little education, secret society member Mahrukh Gawharshinas founded the Taraqqi Girls' School in 1911. As for that open secret: while the public may have known about the Taraqqi Girls' School, Gawharshinas had to keep it secret from her husband, who objected to education for women. When he found out *two years later*, he was livid. Not only did he disapprove, but he also told her she had brought shame upon the family.

She kept the school open anyway.

The first government-run school for girls was finally created in 1918. And now, a little over one hundred years later, women make up 60 percent of university students in Iran.

Fabric of society

Wearing their blue burqas and carrying bags in hand, women entered the Golden Needle Sewing School in Herat, Afghanistan. Once inside, the women pushed aside the scissors and cloth at the top of their bags and pulled out the paper and pens hidden at the bottom. Rather than learning about measuring and cutting, they learned about literature that had been banned. Instead of sharing patterns and fabric, they shared their own stories and poems.

Why the cover-up? For almost twenty years leading up to this moment, Afghanistan had experienced some very difficult times: first the Soviet invasion in 1979, then civil war, and finally the militant Taliban regime taking power in 1996. The Taliban made many changes to the country, including forbidding Afghan women and girls from going to school.

They were, however, allowed to sew. Little did the authorities know this pastime would be the perfect cover, and a small school sign by the door a misleading trick.

That's because the Golden Needle Sewing School wasn't actually a sewing school. It was the home of Mohammed Nasir Rahiyab. Rahiyab was a literature professor at Herat University who believed in the power of words and poetry to offer hope, to lift spirits, to resist. Beginning in 1996, he secretly taught women literature three times a week at his home, while publicly teaching men at the university.

If caught, the teacher and students could have been imprisoned, tortured, or killed. So while Rahiyab's children played outside, they also kept watch so they could warn their father to slip out of the room and the women to replace their writings with their sewing. The Golden Needle Sewing School members weren't the only ones risking their lives to learn and create— hundreds of similar secret schools were active across Herat. Some twenty-nine thousand women and girls bravely attended underground classes over the five years of Taliban rule. (The Taliban were removed from power in 2001, although they would later seize control of the country again in 2021.)

In spite of what they were up against, many women persisted in their studies. One of Rahiyab's students, Leyla Razeghi, wrote two novels and a number of short stories that were published in a literary journal—using a male name instead of her own. After

the Taliban regime fell in 2001, another student, Nadia Anjuman, went on to study literature at Herat University. She also had her writing published, but she used her own name. According to those close to Anjuman, her husband and his family believed her popular book of poetry brought shame on the family, and she was allegedly killed as a result. Her work—which has been translated into multiple languages—is a reminder to Afghan women to keep learning and writing and fighting for their rights.

Born and raised in Herat, Dr. Sakena Yacoobi founded the Afghan Institute of Learning in 1995 to train female teachers and to educate children. After the Taliban regime took over the country, the institute organized eighty secret home schools throughout four provinces of Afghanistan. Approximately three thousand girls were educated in these hidden schools. To avoid suspicion, classes rotated among homes, students arrived and left at different times, and books were hidden in bags of wheat and rice—similar to the secret methods of the Golden Needle Sewing School.

4

SPY SCHOOLS

GOING UNDERGROUND
AND UNDERCOVER

Secret. Covert. Undercover. All of these words might make you think of spies. But they're also words that could describe the schools that *train* the spies used by governments to protect their citizens from outside enemy forces and threats within their own borders.

The art of espionage

The Soviet Union's Committee for State Security—also known as the KGB—was one of the largest and most infamous spy agencies in the world. Its foreign agents (those who worked outside of the Soviet Union) gained access to pretty much every intelligence operation in the Western world and reported back top-secret information. They even went as far as to assassinate state "enemies," both foreign and Soviet.

How did a person become a foreign KGB agent? By attending a spy school hidden in the woods outside the capital city of Moscow. The name of the school depends on who you ask: When it was first created in 1938— some sixteen years before the KGB came to be—it was called the Special Purpose School. Since then, it's been called the Intelligence School, Higher Intelligence School, Red Banner Institute, Andropov Institute ... But whatever its name, the elite school was extremely secretive and its instructors were highly trained and experienced.

Trainees at the concealed campus were given code names based on the first letter of their last name. Code names were used to protect students' identities and to separate their professional from their personal lives. The name "Platov" belonged to the school's most famous graduate— Russian president Vladimir Putin.

As for their studies, they covered everything a spy working for one of the world's most notorious espionage agencies might need to know, including information gathering, making and breaking codes, taking covert photos, secret writing, combat, foreign languages, surveillance, and more.

The program took from one to three years to complete, depending on the trainee's future assignment. But students didn't just have to pass their studies. They also had to pass *being* studied intensely for psychological preparedness, mental sharpness, and physical

endurance—all necessary qualities for a dangerous undercover life working against those considered enemies of the Soviet Union.

In 1991, the once-powerful Soviet Union collapsed and split into fifteen independent countries. That was the end of the KGB. But the spy school still exists with yet a new name—the Academy of Foreign Intelligence.

In 1999, the Central Intelligence Agency (CIA) in the United States released a document titled "Soviet Intelligence Schools in the USSR." The typed document lists Soviet training centers in Estonia, Latvia, Lithuania, and Finland as well as in Moscow dating back to the 1930s. Many entries are scratched out or have handwritten notes alongside, like "military institute of foreign language" or "training schools for agents slated for work in the Far East." There are so many schools listed, the document is fifty-five pages long.

X marks the spot

"A deadly school for dirty warfare." That's how a 2014 documentary described Camp X, a covert World War II spy school. And with good reason: classes at the camp—officially called Special Training School 103—included silent killing, hand-to-hand combat, blowing up railways and bridges, and dodging bullets.

In 1940, the British government created the Special Operations Executive (SOE), an underground volunteer army of secret agents. The SOE needed skilled intelligence agents to go behind enemy lines to sabotage everything from railways to factories to lines of communication. At the time, the island nation was under threat of possible Nazi invasion. Britain needed help—and so it looked across the Atlantic Ocean.

William Stephenson, a Canadian spymaster working for the British government, set up a secret base on farmland near Whitby, Ontario, on the shores of Canada's Lake Ontario. Camp X, the first spy-training facility in North America, opened on December 6, 1941. It was so isolated that locals didn't know it existed. It's been said that even Canadian Prime Minister William Lyon Mackenzie King knew little about it.

For a few weeks up to a few months, recruits from Canada, the United States, and elsewhere came for intense training that included assembling firearms in the dark, setting up trip wire to blow up cars, and shooting the enemy by instinct in a pitch-black firing range. If recruits passed, they went to Britain for "finishing" school. More than five hundred trainees attended Camp X (although it's also been said there were up to two thousand!), with some going on to risk their lives in secret missions during the war.

Without its Canadian neighbors knowing it had ever opened, the Camp X school closed in 1944, after enough agents had been trained and as more European countries were freed from Nazi control. However, the camp's powerful telecommunications center that had sent and received hundreds of thousands of secret messages to and from Britain's famed code breakers at Bletchley Park continued under the Canadian government until 1969. Today, most records have been destroyed or locked away under the fittingly named Official Secrets Act, and the camp buildings have been demolished.

- In 1944, Canadian agent and former Camp X trainee Leonard Jacques Taschereau landed in France with his team and planted bombs on twenty-two German-run locomotives—all in one night! The next year, he was honored with the Military Cross for his tremendous service.

- British major Paul Dehn was a political warfare instructor at Camp X and cowrote the school's training manual, but he's most famous as an Oscar-winning screenwriter who wrote the film *Goldfinger*, featuring dashing and daring superspy James Bond.

Word for word

"Friends" is not exactly how one would describe the relationship between the United States and the Soviet Union during World War II, even if they were allies. And after the war, things got worse: their dislike for and mistrust of each other deepened, leading to the Cold War—a tense, decades-long political standoff.

Fearing the Soviet Union's growing power and the threat of a nuclear war, Britain sided with the United States. But to defeat the enemy, you have to know the enemy, and not many British citizens spoke Russian. So in 1951, by order of the British prime minister, the top-secret Joint Services School for Linguists (JSSL) was created.

At the time, all healthy, young British men had to serve in the military. Some of the brightest were sent to secret JSSL locations for intense language training so they could learn the skills needed to listen in on, translate, and interpret Russian communications that could potentially signal military threat or invasion.

Studying at JSSL—which held classes in different locations around England and Scotland—was far from easy. It was intense and demanding—more pressure than any regular school because a simple misunderstanding could leave the world open to some serious danger. Trainees were taught Russian language, culture, and history by trusted Soviet fugitives and defectors. (Some students also learned Polish and Czech.) They studied grammar, memorized thirty new words a day, learned to speak and read Russian, and were taught to translate from Russian to English and from English

Spy school … theater? Some of the JSSL teachers hired to drum the Russian language into their students did so with creativity and flair:

- Polycarpe Pavloff and Vera Grech were a married couple and former actors with the Moscow Art Theatre who had arrived in Paris with their touring company—and stayed. They staged classic Russian plays, such as Anton Chekhov's *The Cherry Orchard* and *Three Sisters*, with their JSSL students.
- Theater lovers Dmitri Makaroff and Vladimir Koshevnikoff wrote, translated, directed, and occasionally starred in classical and religious plays in Russian using trainees as the cast. Their JSSL Shakespearean productions included *Hamlet*, *Othello*, and *Twelfth Night*.

to Russian. They had to know the Russian words for things they'd never known even in English, like every part of a tank. There were also regular tests and exams. And if they failed … they were out.

More than four thousand servicemen were trained as Cold War Russian translators and interpreters. The work could be dangerous, especially for those who tried to intercept messages by "accidentally" flying into enemy airspace or drifting into enemy waters. But many others sat in windowless rooms crammed with electronic equipment, recording bits and pieces of information that didn't seem to make much sense. Yet when those bits and pieces were deciphered and linked, patterns emerged and knowledge of Soviet military operations grew.

By 1960, mandatory military duty ended in Britain and the special-language spy school was closed. But a number of trainees had developed such a love for Russian that they enrolled not so secretly in related courses at university!

5

RADICAL LEARNING

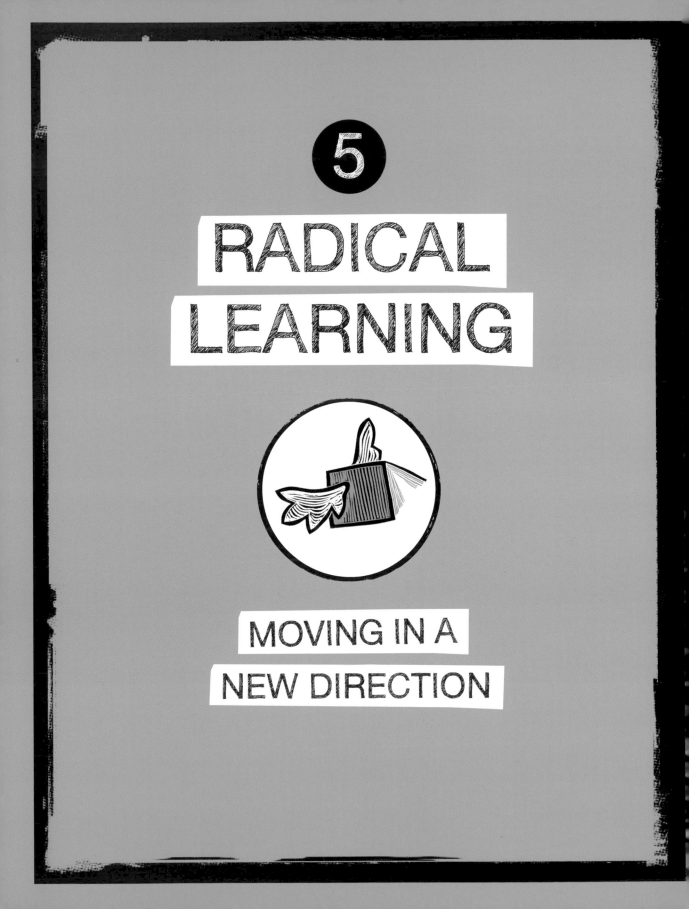

MOVING IN A NEW DIRECTION

What do you do when you don't agree with your country's government, your local school system, or a group's militant instruction? From student-led study circles to an experimental educational approach to a government-run program for the children of violent extremists, people have set up secret schools as a step toward making the changes they want to see for generations to come.

Talking in circles

Just like in many countries around the world, students across South Korea enter university to study medicine, music, engineering, business, and more. But in the 1980s, another kind of higher learning was happening—one taking place underground.

These were covert classes that weren't organized by the universities or taught by the universities' professors. They were run by students for students. And they needed to be secret because the messages being passed along could be considered against the law.

Older university students would invite younger ones to secret "study circles" or "reading groups" where they learned about political theories and revolutionary movements in the Soviet Union, Cuba, and China. They talked about the problems in South Korea, the United States' influence on South Korean politics, and the need to reunite with North Korea. (After World War II, Korea was split in two, with the Soviet Union occupying North Korea and the United States remaining in South Korea.)

Students attending the underground classes were being recruited into a pro-democracy movement that was sweeping campuses across the country. The movement was calling for changes, especially for an end to South Korea's new military rule. Almost a quarter of a million student protesters and their allies took to the streets in the city of Gwangju in May 1980, and the resulting Gwangju Uprising turned bloody and brutal when government soldiers moved in. Even though media coverage of the uprising was censored, study circle members got hold of film footage and pictures of the resulting massacre.

Although student activism has long been a part of South Korean history, it took an urgent turn after Gwangju. The movement kept growing, and in 1985, half a million students participated in more than two thousand protests—that's more than five protests per day!

But the underground students and protesters continued to see violence, arrests, and tear gas.

And then, on June 9, 1987, a student protester demonstrating against another student's torture and death was hit in the head by a police tear gas canister (he would later die from the injury). This event, among others, helped fuel a massive twenty-day demonstration that spread across South Korea. Millions of people took to the streets to protest against the military dictatorship during what became known as the June Struggle. With the world watching because the Olympic Summer Games in Seoul were

just one year away, the government accepted the people's demands and the road to democracy was paved.

The Korean student movement and its secret study circles had effected powerful public change.

South Korean physics student Kim Song-man studied for a year at Western Illinois University in the United States. He returned to South Korea in 1983. In 1985, he was arrested and sentenced to death for allegedly setting up study circles, spying for Communist North Korea, and passing around literature about North Korea to students. Amnesty International called Kim a "prisoner of conscience," meaning he had been imprisoned for his beliefs. After two years on death row and thirteen years in prison, Kim was finally released.

Rocketing to new heights

At the SpaceX headquarters near Los Angeles, California, kids battled with robots and debated the pros and cons of artificial intelligence. But they weren't on a field trip to the space exploration company. They were students in a secret school called Ad Astra, meaning "to the stars."

Elon Musk—the billionaire CEO of SpaceX and electric carmaker Tesla—has long been considered a technology rebel. But in 2014, he set his revolutionary sights on a much different project: school.

As the father of school-age children, he was unhappy with traditional curriculum and teaching methods, which he himself had disliked while growing up. Educators had students memorizing information and formulas without actually explaining *why* they needed to know this stuff.

Believing there had to be a better way, he quietly created a nonprofit, experimental school for his five sons and a few other high-achieving children. The focus was on math, science, engineering, computer science, and ethics. There were no grades and few assignments. But there was lots of hands-on learning. Students worked in teams and chose projects they wanted to create, subjects they wanted to research, and problems they wanted to solve. Basically, they were encouraged to pursue their passions, work to their abilities, and physically take things apart in order to understand abstract ideas and theories.

Although the unconventional school was supersecret when it began in 2014, word of the school eventually got out. By 2017, some four hundred families had applied for a dozen open spots for children ages seven to fourteen. Still, the information about and admissions process to Ad Astra remained low-key. There was a basic website, an application form, and three challenging questions to answer. One admission question, for example, asked potential students to determine the three best and worst planets for humanity to live on and explain why. The anti-establishment school that began with just eight students gathering in an office conference room had classrooms and a lab for upward of forty students by 2018.

Some critics of Ad Astra picked on what was missing from the curriculum: classes in languages, music, and sports. Others wondered what would happen to the school when Musk's own kids finished. For Musk, the thing that mattered most was the students. "The kids really love going to school," he shared during a Beijing Television interview. "I think that's a good sign."

Ad Astra is now closed. But the team behind it, including its cofounder Joshua Dahn, formed a new school open to "kind, creative, and academically ambitious students" between the ages of ten and fourteen for remote learning from anywhere in the world. The new school's name? Astra Nova, or "new star."

Beyond belief

Tucked away in the Indonesian capital of Jakarta is a secret school for children of suicide bombers. The students aren't learning how to become militants like their parents, though. Quite the opposite: this school is trying to reverse the radical teachings that have been handed down to them. The aim is to protect the children from becoming the next generation of terrorists, to give them a chance at a normal life.

Indonesia is home to many religions, including the world's largest Muslim population. A small number of Muslim Indonesians believe in a very strict interpretation of Islamic law—some to the extreme. A few have even carried out a series of suicide bombings targeting the "enemies" of Islam, including religious minorities and law enforcement, in order to create a political-religious Islamic state.

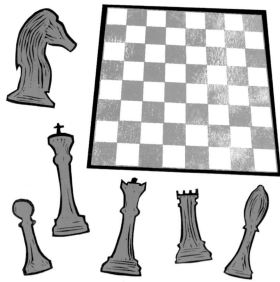

Because of their parents' actions, the children of these Islamic militants are at higher risk of being bullied and ostracized at regular schools, leading them to drop out. To keep children from returning to the militant life they grew up in, the Indonesian government created a new kind of school for them.

The fifteen-month program has no more than a dozen students at a time. And just as the location of the school is a secret, so are the children's names— they all have nicknames to protect their identities, even from each other.

Social workers at the secret school provide psychological and social counseling to the students, some of whom witnessed their parents' acts of terrorism. The children learn about Indonesian history and heroes, about tolerance and free will, and about how Islam is about love and mercy. They are encouraged to make friends and play with one another.

Although the program is still new, there are signs of its success: children listen to music, dance, and draw pictures of living creatures—pastimes that had been forbidden by their Islamic militant parents. One young girl who once dreamed of being a martyr like her parents, who were willing to die for their cause, now dreams of being a teacher.

Khairul Ghazali was sent to prison for terrorism-related crimes. After being released in 2015, he opened the Al-Hidayah Islamic Boarding School in North Sumatra, Indonesia, for the children of imprisoned or killed militants. The aim of the school is to reverse radical teachings passed down to the students from their guardians or parents; teach the true meaning of Islam; and provide regular classes, activities, and life skills. The school works with up to twenty-five students at a time, some of whom now aspire to be teachers and police officers. But according to Ghazali, there are still thousands of children across the country who need similar support.

Conclusion

Education is such a powerful tool that many people have faced death, risked punishment, crossed borders, defied laws, confronted social norms, and hid from authorities—all to attend secret schools.

Think about how covert classes that taught reading and writing often provided a lifeline to freedom for the enslaved in the United States. Or how South Korean university students sat in on underground study circles to learn about their country's pro-democracy movement. Or how trainees from across North America traveled to a spy camp in Canada to secretly learn how to sabotage the Nazis.

Then there's what it means to be part of a community, to be around others in a similar situation. Classrooms become not only places of learning but in some cases safe spaces. Consider the children in Indonesia whose secret schooling is striving to help lessen trauma and conflict, or the women in Afghanistan whose "sewing" classes were a way to fight gender inequality. Schools can also maintain and promote cultural ancestry in the face of adversity, as they did for Indigenous children in Ecuador and Japanese children in Brazil.

Being in school can also make the world a better place, even if for just a short while, like for the Jewish children in the Nazi ghettos whose underground lessons gave them temporary relief from the horrors going on around them. Hope fueled the teachers who ran the secret schools. Hope fueled the students who attended.

The schools you've read about are not just stories. They did and do exist. And for every secret school we've learned about, there are certainly more that will remain hidden forever.

Notes

12/13 "Just as the sun ... lords and servants." Dolores Cacuango, quoted in *Indigenous Knowledge and Practices in Education in Latin America: Exploratory Analysis of How Indigenous Cultural Worldviews and Concepts Influence Regional Educational Policy*, (OREAL/UNESCO Santiago, 2017). Online.

16/17 "Knowledge ... freedom." Frederick Douglass, *The Life and Times of Frederick Douglass* (Hartford, CT: Park Publishing, 1881), 71.

20/21 "Education ... the world." Nelson Mandela, quoted in *Oxford Essential Quotations*, ed. Susan Ratcliffe, 5th ed. (Oxford University Press, 2017). Online.

26/27 "Women's education ... family." Unnamed, quoted in Muhammad Sahimi, "Iranian Women and the Struggle for Democracy: 1. The Pre-Revolution Era," *PBS Frontline*, April 15, 2010. Online.

34/35 "A deadly school for dirty warfare." Michael Allcock, narrator, quoted in *Camp X: Secret Agent School,* History, aired July 14, 2014.

42/43 "The kids ... good sign." Elon Musk, interviewed in "Elon Musk Talks about a New Type of School He Created for His Kids 2015," Beijing Television, uploaded to YouTube by Elon Musk Best Videos, November 30, 2015. Online.

42/43 "Kind ... students." "Apply" webpage, the Astra Nova School website, accessed December 30, 2020. Online.

Selected Bibliography

Section 1: Cultural Connections
Becker, Marc, editor. *Indigenous and Afro-Ecuadorians Facing the Twenty-First Century*. Newcastle upon Tyne, UK: Cambridge Scholars Publishing, 2013.

De Carvalho, Daniela. *Migrants and Identity in Japan and Brazil: The Nikkeijin*. London: RoutledgeCurzon, 2003.

Girnius, Saulius A. "Bishop Motiejus Valančius, a Man for All Seasons." *Lituanus: Lithuanian Quarterly Journal of Arts and Science 2, vol. 22, no. 2, Summer 1976*. Online.

González Terreros, María Isabel. "Las escuelas clandestinas en Ecuador. Raíces de la educación indígena intercultural." *Revista Colombiana de Educación, no. 69, 2015, pp.* 75–95. Online.

Kosminsky, Ethel V. *An Ethnography of the Lives of Japanese and Japanese Brazilian Migrants: Childhood, Family, and Work*. Lanham, MD: Lexington Books, 2020.

Section 2: Hope and Dignity
Brand, Christo, and Barbara Jones. *Mandela: My Prisoner, My Friend*. New York: Thomas Dunne Books, 2014.

Buntman, Fran Lisa. *Robben Island and Prisoner Resistance to Apartheid*. New York: Cambridge University Press, 2003.

Goldman Rubin, Susan. *Fireflies in the Dark: The Story of Friedl Dicker-Brandeis and the Children of Terezin*. New York: Holiday House, 2000.

Jacobs Altman, Linda. *Warsaw, Lodz, Vilna: The Holocaust Ghettos*. Berkeley Heights, NJ: Enslow Publishers, 2015.

Williams, Heather Andrea. *Self-Taught: African American Education in Slavery and Freedom*. Chapel Hill: University of North Carolina Press, 2005.

Section 3: Girls' Rights
Childress, Diana. *Equal Rights Is Our Minimum Demand: The Women's Rights Movement in Iran, 2005*. Minneapolis: Twenty-First Century Books, 2011.

Lamb, Christina. *The Sewing Circles of Herat: A Personal Voyage Through Afghanistan*. New York: HarperCollins Publishers, 2002.

Lifton, Betty Jean. *The King of Children: The Life and Death of Janusz Korczak*. New York: Farrar, Straus and Giroux, 1988.

Sahimi, Muhammad. "Iranian Women and the Struggle for Democracy: 1. The Pre-Revolution Era." *PBS Frontline*, April 15, 2010. Online.

Waldman, Amy. "A Nation Challenged: Culture; Afghan Poets Revive Literary Tradition." *New York Times*, December 16, 2001. Online.

Section 4: Spy Schools
Camp-X official site. Accessed January 2, 2021. Online.

Elliott, Geoffrey, and Harold Shukman. *Secret Classrooms: An Untold Story of the Cold War*. London: Faber & Faber, 2013. Kindle edition.

Myers, Steven Lee. *The New Tsar: The Rise and Reign of Vladimir Putin*. New York: Vintage Books, 2016.

Pringle, Robert W. "KGB. "*Encyclopaedia Britannica*. Accessed January 2, 2021. Online.

Stafford, David. "Camp X."*The Canadian Encyclopedia*, Historica Canada. February 7, 2006. Last modified August 1, 2018. Online.

Section 5: Radical Learning
Beech, Hannah, and Muktita Suhartono. "At a School for Suicide Bombers' Children, Dancing, Drawing and Deradicalization." *New York Times*, October 18, 2019. Online.

Harris, Mark. "First Space, Then Auto—Now Elon Musk Quietly Tinkers with Education." *Ars Technica*, June 25, 2018. Online.

Park, Mi. *Democracy and Social Change: A History of South Korean Student Movements, 1980–2000*. Bern, Switzerland: Peter Lang, 2008.

"'Victims and Perpetrators': Rehabilitating Indonesia's Child Bombers." Agence France-Presse, July 12, 2019. Online.